Most plants have seeds.

When you put a seed in the ground and water it,

a new plant grows from it.

Seeds often travel to faraway places.
If seeds did not travel, too many plants would grow
in one place. It would be very crowded!

Some seeds travel on the wind.

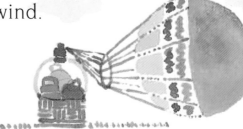

Some seeds travel in the water.

Many seeds travel inside fruits.

The fruit is like a suitcase for the seeds.
It protects them on their trip.

Fruits look beautiful and taste good, so animals and people eat them . . .

. . . and drop the seeds in different places.

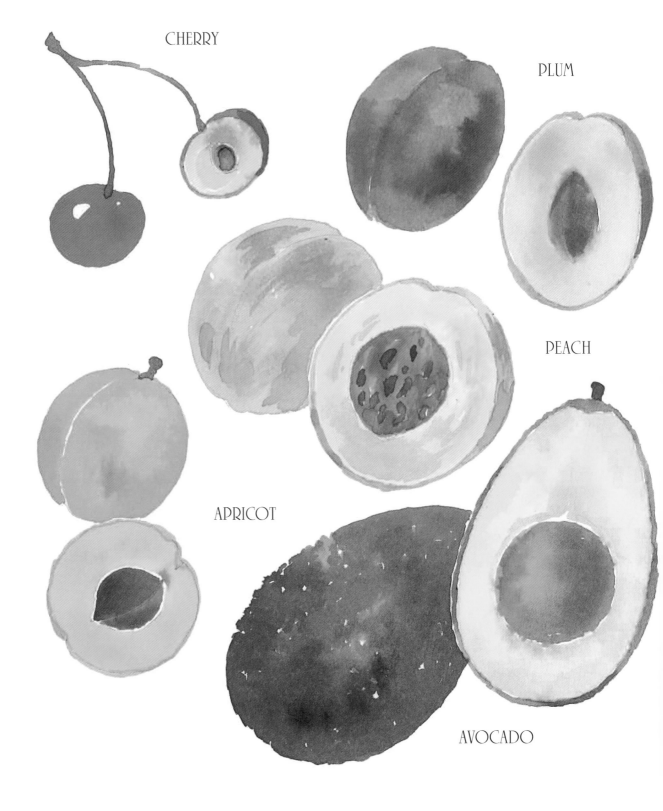

CHERRY

PLUM

PEACH

APRICOT

AVOCADO

Some fruits carry one big seed inside them.
The seed is called a pit.

A cherry is one of these fruits.

LEMON

MELON

APPLE

PEAR

Some fruits have many small seeds inside them.

An apple is one of these fruits.

BANANA

KIWI

BLUEBERRY

Some fruits have many, many tiny seeds inside them.

A kiwi is one of these fruits.

Many berries, such as strawberries and blackberries,
carry their seeds on the outside!

Raspberries do too.

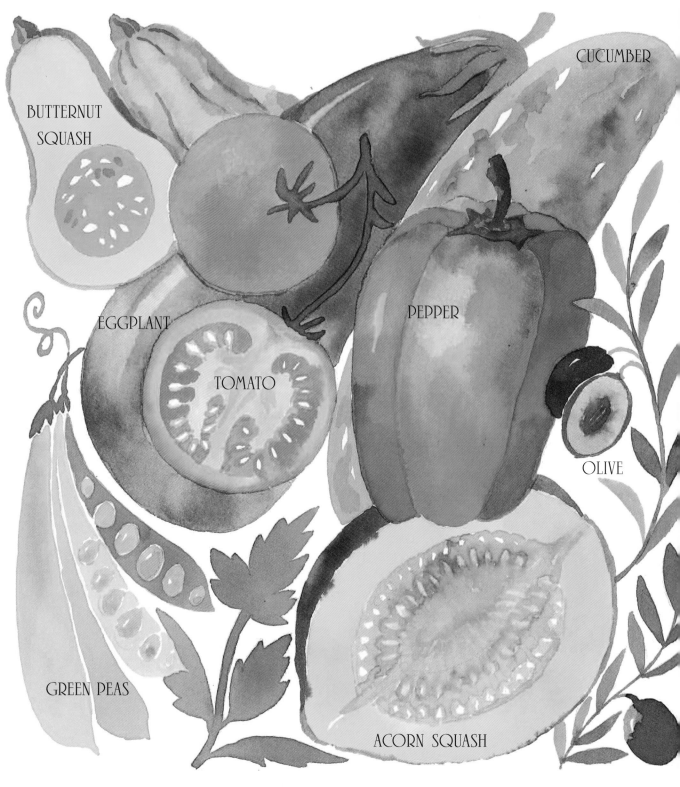

BUTTERNUT
SQUASH

CUCUMBER

EGGPLANT

TOMATO

PEPPER

OLIVE

GREEN PEAS

ACORN SQUASH

Some vegetables we eat are really fruits.
They carry seeds too.

Peas are seeds.

Can you find the seeds on this ear of corn?

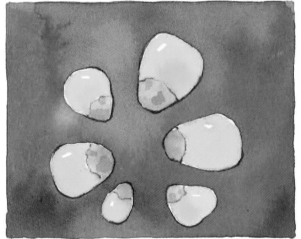
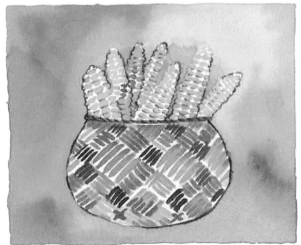

Hint: It's the part you eat.

I'll bet you didn't know that every time you
eat a peach, a cherry, an avocado, a plum, a cucumber,
a tomato, a grape,

an apple, an orange, a pea, a pear, a melon,
a banana, or a blueberry,

you're really eating a suitcase . . .

. . . a suitcase for seeds!

Questions and Answers for
A Fruit Is a Suitcase for Seeds

Q: What's the difference between a fruit and a vegetable?

A: Fruits and vegetables are parts of plants. A vegetable can be the leaf (spinach), the root (carrot), or even the flower (broccoli). A fruit (apples, cherries, peaches) is the part of a plant that holds the seeds. But some vegetables hold seeds, too (cucumbers, tomatoes, green peppers). Are these vegetables really fruits? There is no clear answer to this question. Maybe we should think of them as both!

Q: Do all fruits come from flowers?

A: Yes. All fruits develop from flowers. That's true for vegetables that hold seeds, too.

Q: Why don't seeds grow in your tummy?

A: Small seeds that you swallow when you eat a tomato or a slice of cucumber can't grow inside you. Seeds need earth, water, light, and air to grow. They can't get those things inside a person. The seeds you eat go out of your body when you poop.

Q: What's the biggest seed in the world?

A: The biggest seed weighs about as much as a five-year old (about 45 pounds or 20 kilograms). It grows on a special palm tree called the Double Coconut tree.

Q: What's the smallest seed in the world?

A: The smallest seeds belong to the orchid flower family. They are so tiny you can hardly see them. One million of these seeds would weigh as much as one grape.

Q: Do big seeds grow into big plants or trees, and little seeds into little ones?

A: No. The size of the seed makes no difference. The biggest tree in the world, the giant redwood, which grow as high as a thirty-story building, grows from a seed that is smaller than the head of an ant.

Q: Can you grow a plant from a seed at home?

A: Sure. Take a flowerpot filled with earth, put it on a saucer, and poke a seed down into the earth with your finger. Pour some water on it and put it in a sunny place. Add some water every couple of days so it doesn't dry out.

Good seeds to plant are any kind of dried beans or citrus seeds from oranges, grapefruits, or lemons. Make sure you pick the fat citrus seeds and let them dry out for a week or so before you plant them. The beans should come up in a few days. The citrus seeds take two or three weeks.

Helpful hint: If you don't have a yard to dig up the dirt, you can buy a bag of potting soil at the store.

If you want to see how a seed sprouts, put a few dried lentils on some wet cotton in a bowl or saucer. Cover it with plastic wrap and put it on a windowsill. In a few days, when the little white roots and the tiny green stems start to grow, you can plant them (root down!) in a flower pot, just like the beans or citrus seeds.

Then just sit back and wait.

About the Author
and Illustrator

Jean Richards, an actress, has been involved with children's books not only as a writer but also as a performer. She has recorded more than two hundred children's tapes and records. A resident of New York City, Ms. Richard's Broadway credits include *Fiddler on the Roof* and *The Rothschilds*.

Anca Hariton was trained as an architect at the University of Bucharest, a profession that she still practices when she is not illustrating children's books. Ms. Hariton lives in Richmond, California.